~ Darcey ~

Have fun with words!

Alicia Ward~Jarrow

Alicia Ward-Yarrow is an actor, musician, composer and teacher. She plays the piano and violin and studied music at Dartington College of Arts in Devon. This was followed by postgraduate studies at Middlesex University. Alicia runs music, drama and dance workshops, promoting confidence, communication skills and social wellbeing among children and young people. She lives in Sunderland and regularly plays in a local northeast orchestra and an Irish ceili band.

TWENTY-SIX
Terrifically Terrifying, Twirling, Tantalising, Tiptop, Toe-Tapping TONGUE-TWISTERS!

Words and illustrations
by Alicia Ward-Yarrow

The Printing House

For
Harriet, Eliot,
Thomas and James

A

Agile Agatha the acrobatic alligator

acknowledged the astonished, ambidextrous antelope.

B

The baffled baboon
bounced the balloon

to the badger
playing the bagpipes.

The camel
with the
collywobbles
carried the
custard
carefully,

C

but crashed into
the clever clown,
clattering his castanets!

D

The dancing daisies
dazzled the dizzy dandelions.

Eliza the elegant and
effervescent elephant

liked to examine
    the exciting encyclopaedia.

F

Forty-five flowery fairies
danced the fancy foxtrot

to the fast
and flashy,
flowing music
of the fabulous,
fascinating fiddle.

'The greedy, grumpy goat gobbled the grass in the garden,'

gabbled the giggling girl as she gaped at the glittering galaxy.

H

Hector the happy, hiccupping hedgehog

hurried to help Harry the hula-hooping hippopotamus.

I see indigo icicles
inside the igloo

where the indulgent iguana
has his eye on the ice cream.

J

The jumping Jeep jingled
and the jolly, juicy jelly jangled.

K

The karate-kicking kangaroo

caught the kaleidoscopic kite
and kept the key for the kennel
by the kettle in the kitchen.

L

The little, lucky ladybird
left a little, lemon lollipop

for the lively, laughing lamb
who lolloped along the lane.

The mischievous monkey merrily muttered to the magnificent magician making meringues:

'We must march many miles to the mysterious maze to marvel at the melodious music.'

N

Never go near the
notorious nettle –

it's nasty

and nothing
but a nuisance.

Octavia the octopus
was often optimistic
and objected to every obstacle
that obstructed the orchestra,

but the otter and the ostrich
were outrageously outspoken
and the outburst that they offered
was just obviously too obnoxious!

P

The panther popped the ping-pong
as he passed the precious parcel
to the pleasant panda playing
a polka upon the piano.

Q

There was
quarrelling and
quibbling,
quivering and
quaking,

as the quality
of the quiche
did not qualify
to serve the Queen.

R

'It's rock 'n' roll!'
raved the rocking radio
with a rondo rhythm
and a rattling reel!

The rhinoceros raced,
the rabbit ran
to the roly-poly rhapsody
at Rendezvous Road!

'The skipping squirrel squabbled at the scarecrow's secret scherzo,'

sang the swishing, swooping, sweeping swan, serenely singing a song.

T

The tiny, talented,
tartan teddy
got tangled in the tango,

tapped on the tambourine
and trotted on the trampoline.

The table toppled,
the trifle trickled,
the tutti-frutti tripled
and the treacle toffee tickled.

𝒰

There were
umpteen umpires
unaware of the unicorn,

underneath the umbrella
in his unique uniform.

V

The viola and the violin
have very vivacious voices.
The vital volume of these virtuosos
is varied, valued and vivid.

The weary walrus waltzed,
whilst whistling wonderfully well.

Whoops!

... After a whirl he wobbled!

Whoopee!

... After a wobble he whirled!

Exuberant Xenia,
though exhausted and exasperated,
expertly excelled
on the exhilarating xylophone.

Y

You
yo-yoed
your
yo-yo
then yelled
'Yahoo!'
After a yarn you yawned
then yodelled and yelped.

Z

The zebra was so zealous
that he zoomed in a zigzag zone.

Then he zipped
down to zero
to play his zither
with zest at the zoo.